10/11

WITHAM

Lions

by Helen Orme

D0238933

**Essex County
Council Libraries**

Copyright © ticktock Entertainment Ltd 2006
First published in Great Britain in 2006 by ticktock Media Ltd.,
Unit 2, Orchard Business Centre, North Farm Road,
Tunbridge Wells, Kent, TN2 3XF
ISBN 1 86007 964 4 pbk
Printed in Hong Kong
A CIP catalogue record for this book is available from the British Library.
All rights reserved. No part of this publication may be reproduced, copied, stored in a retrieval
system or transmitted in any form or by any means electronic, mechanical, photocopying,
recording or otherwise without prior written permission of the copyright owner.

Picture credits
t=top, b=bottom, c=centre, l-left, r=right
Alamy: 6-7, 11c, 14-15, 17c, 24b, 31. Corbis: 4-5, 8, 9, 10-11, 12-13, 16, 17b, 20-21, 25, 26t, 27, 28, 29, 32.
Oxford Scientific Photo Library: 18-19. Superstock: 22-23.

Every effort has been made to trace the copyright holders, and we apologise in advance for any unintentional omissions.
We would be pleased to insert the appropriate acknowledgements in any subsequent edition of this publication.

CONTENTS

Words that appear **in bold** are explained in the glossary.

THE GRASSLANDS OF AFRICA

*Life isn't easy for animals on the **grasslands** of Africa.*

At some times of year, there is heavy rain. At other times, it is as dry as in a desert.

Huge numbers of animals live on the grasslands. Antelopes and zebras eat the tough grass. Giraffes feed on the thorny trees.

Many **predators** live in this **habitat**, such as cheetahs, leopards, and the largest grassland predator – the lion.

THE PRIDE

A family of lions is called a pride.

The pride may have many females, called lionesses, but only between one and four males.

When young male lions are two to four years old they will leave their pride. Sometimes they will stay together in male groups.

When they are old enough, male lions look for a pride of their own to take over.

MALE LIONS

Male lions are bigger than females, and their **manes** *make them look even bigger.*

Adult male lions are in charge of the pride. They guard the pride's **territory** and keep the group safe.

Males leave their scent on trees and rocks, and roar loudly to warn other lions to stay away.

A male lion will lead his pride until a younger and fitter male fights him and takes over.

All lions have black hairs at the end of their tails.

LION CUBS

*Lionesses will have two to four cubs at one time. They give birth in a **den**, hidden away in rocks or long grass.*

Cubs feed on their mother's milk until they are six months old. When they are about six weeks old they will start to eat some meat caught by their mother.

The females in a pride share the job of looking after the cubs.

MUMS AND BABIES FACT

Lionesses carry their cubs in their mouths.

HUNTING FOR FOOD

Lions will hunt at any time, but they prefer to hunt at night.

The lionesses do most of the hunting. Male lions are big and heavy and not as fast as the females.

Lions get some of their food by **scavenging**. They look for animals that have died, or have been killed by another predator.

NIGHT VISION

Lions can see in the dark six times better than a human!

MAKING WAY FOR PEOPLE

Life is becoming tougher for the lions of Africa. They are having to make way for people.

Some of these people are miners looking for **minerals** and metals in the ground.

When the miners find valuable minerals, large areas of grassland can be destroyed or **polluted**.

Local lions may be seen as a danger to workers and shot.

LIONS AND FARMERS

*In the African countries where lions live the human **populations** are growing.*

Towns are spreading and more and more of the grasslands are becoming farmland.

Without the grasslands, **prey animals**, such as zebra and antelopes, will disappear. Hungry lions will attack farm animals if they have no prey animals to hunt.

Many lions are shot by farmers who do not want lions killing their cattle.

TROPHY HUNTING

Hunting lions as sport is allowed in some places in Africa. Hunters kill the animals, especially males, so that they can have a dead lion as a trophy.

THE ASIATIC LION

If the African lions are not helped they could be in as much danger as their cousins the Asiatic lions.

Around 200 years ago, the Asiatic lion was found from India all the way to Europe.

Now, because of hunting and habitat destruction, there are fewer than 300 Asiatic lions left in the world.

The only place they live wild is in the Gir National Park in India.

ASIA

Gir National Park

Asiatic lions are smaller than African lions, and the males have smaller manes.

A SAFE HOME FOR LIONS

The best way to make sure that lions have a future is to find them a safe place to live.

In Africa, some countries have set up **wildlife reserves**. It is against the law to hunt animals in the reserves.

Wardens protect the animals and make sure that there is enough grassland to feed prey animals, such as antelopes and zebras.

Lions can be brought into the reserves from places where they are not safe.

DO LIONS HAVE A FUTURE?

The future of the lions depends on people.

It might seem a bad idea to bring **tourists** into the wildlife reserves to look at lions. But the lions soon get used to visitors.

Wildlife tourists spend money which helps make jobs for the people who live in or near the reserves. This means that protecting the lions and other wild animals is important to local people.

Farmers who live in the area also understand that they must share the reserve with the lions.

FACTFILE

THE WORLD OF THE AFRICAN LION

African lions live on grasslands in the red areas on the map.

AFRICA

Atlantic Ocean

Sahara Desert

AFRICA

• Lions are doing well if they live in wildlife reserves. But in other areas, lions are disappearing fast.

Animals of the grasslands

Predators: lions, leopards, cheetahs and hyenas.

Prey animals: buffaloes, wildebeests, antelopes, giraffes, zebras and warthogs.

Elephants chase a pride of lions away from a waterhole.

LION BODIES

In the wild, lions can live to be 18 years old, but most die before they reach the age of 10.

• A male lion has a mane to make him look big and scary to other males.

• The mane also protects the lion when he fights.

Male
Length: up to 3 m (including tail)
Weight: up to 240 kg

Female
Length: up to 2.5 m (including tail)
Weight: up to 180 kg

• When cubs are born, they have light spots or stripes on their coats. These fade away when the cubs are about three months old.

25

HOW MANY AFRICAN LIONS?

There are between 17,000 and 23,000 lions living wild in Africa. This is about half the number there were fifty years ago.

There are just 300 Asiatic lions living wild in India.

PROBLEMS FOR LIONS

• The population of Africa is growing and in some places the people do not have enough to eat. The lions' habitat is disappearing as people need more land to grow food and keep cattle.

• Farmers shoot lions, if the lions attack their cattle.

• Lions are still hunted in some parts of Africa for sport. Sometimes, they are trapped in pens and hunters are allowed to shoot them. This is called *canned hunting* and it is very cruel because the lions have no chance to escape.

FACTFILE

CONSERVATION

• **Conservation** groups and governments set up wildlife reserves for lions and their prey animals. The reserves need to protect the whole habitat because all living things depend on each other to live.

• Wildlife reserves must be good for local people as well as the animals and plants. If the reserves give people jobs and money, they will want to look after the wild animals and their habitats.

• The best way to bring in money to the reserves is to welcome wildlife tourists. This must be done carefully so the animals are not disturbed.

• Sometimes big cats such as lions and leopards are kept in poorly run zoos or as attractions in circuses. Conservation groups try to rescue these animals and find them new homes in special wildlife reserves where they can be protected and live a wild life!

HOW YOU CAN HELP THE LIONS

•Find out about lions and other animals in danger. Do a project or a display at your school to tell other people about them.

• Join an organisation like the *World Wildlife Fund* or the *Born Free Foundation*. These groups need to raise money to pay for their conservation work. You could organise an event to help raise funds – try having a sale of all your unwanted clothes, old toys and books! See the websites below for lots of fundraising ideas.

• Find out about schemes that let you adopt a lion. (Don't worry; it won't be coming to live with you!) Maybe your school could do this. Go to the *Born Free Foundation* website to find out how.

Visit these websites for more information and to find out how you can help to 'Save the lions'.

Born Free Foundation: www.bornfree.org.uk
World Wildlife Fund International: www.wwf.org.uk
African Wildlife Foundation: www.awf.org
Asiatic Lion Information Centre: www.asiatic-lion.org

GLOSSARY

carnivores Animals that eat meat.

conservation Taking care of the natural world.

den An animal's home, or a hidden place where an animal sleeps or has its babies.

grasslands Dry areas covered with grass where only a few bushes and trees grow.

habitat A place in the wild that suits a particular animal or plant.

manes The long hair around the necks of male lions.

minerals Valuable substances, such as gold or platinum, found in the earth.

polluted Damaged by rubbish, or by chemicals and oils that have escaped onto the land.

populations The people who live in particular places or countries.

predators Animals that live by killing and eating other animals.

prey animals Animals that are hunted by other animals for food.

scavenging Looking for meat that other predators have left, or from animals that are already dead.

territory The area in which an animal or a family of animals lives.

tourists People who are on holiday.

wardens People whose job it is to look after protected reserves and the animals that live there.

wildlife reserves Places set aside for wild animals and plants to live. The animals and their habitat are protected by laws.

INDEX